BRONCHITIS EDUCATION FOR HEALTHCARE PROVIDERS

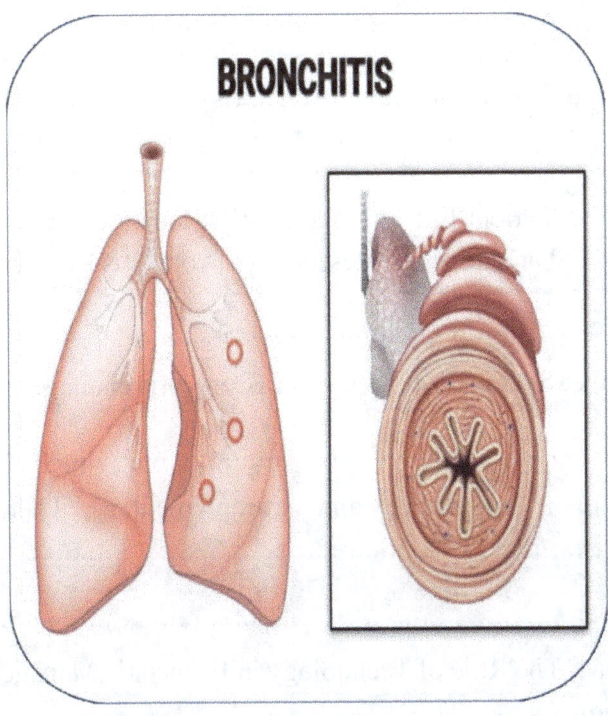

TABLE OF CONTENTS

COURSE OVERVIEW

This course offers an in-depth exploration of bronchitis, designed specifically for healthcare professionals including respiratory therapists, doctors, and nurses. The curriculum covers both acute and chronic bronchitis, emphasizing clinical and physiological signs, diagnostic imaging, treatment protocols, and patient education. Participants will gain a thorough understanding of bronchitis management through a blend of theoretical knowledge and practical applications. The course also addresses the role of technology in bronchitis care, integrative and complementary therapies, and special considerations for different patient populations.

COURSE OBJECTIVES:

By the end of this course, participants will be able to Understand the Pathophysiology of Bronchitis, Recognize Clinical and Physiological Signs, Utilize Diagnostic Tools, Develop Treatment Plans, Educate Patients and Promote Self-Management, Address Special Populations, Integrate Complementary Therapies, Leverage Technology in Care, Stay Informed on Emerging Trends, Collaborate Effectively Collaborate Effectively. This course aims to equip healthcare providers with the knowledge and skills necessary to deliver high-quality, patient-centered care to individuals affected by bronchitis, ultimately improving patient outcomes and enhancing the overall management of this common respiratory condition.

COURSE MATERIALS

To learn this course, **healthcare providers/ participants** must be provided with materials like a Pen, pencil, notebook, and notepad to better understand and make it easy for them to learn.

INTRODUCTION

Bronchitis, a common respiratory condition, is characterized by inflammation of the bronchial tubes, which carry air to and from the lungs. For healthcare providers, understanding the intricacies of bronchitis is crucial for effective diagnosis, treatment, and patient management. This book, "Comprehensive Bronchitis Education for Healthcare Providers: From Diagnosis to Treatment," aims to serve as an exhaustive resource for respiratory therapists, doctors, nurses, and other healthcare professionals dedicated to respiratory care.

The primary goal of this book is to provide an in-depth exploration of bronchitis, covering every aspect from its basic definition to the latest treatment protocols. By delving into the clinical signs, physiological manifestations, and diagnostic imaging techniques, healthcare providers can gain a comprehensive understanding of how bronchitis presents in patients. This knowledge is vital for distinguishing bronchitis from other respiratory conditions with similar symptoms. "Comprehensive Bronchitis Education for Healthcare Providers: From Diagnosis to Treatment" is designed to be an essential reference for any healthcare professional involved in respiratory care. By covering all aspects of bronchitis in detail, this book aims to enhance the proficiency of healthcare providers in diagnosing, treating, and managing this common yet complex condition. Through this comprehensive guide, readers will be better equipped to deliver high-quality care to patients suffering from bronchitis.

MODULE ONE

LESSON ONE: UNDERSTANDING BRONCHITIS

Bronchitis is a condition characterized by inflammation of the bronchial tubes, which are responsible for carrying air to and from the lungs. This inflammation leads to symptoms such as coughing, mucus production, and difficulty breathing. There are two primary types of bronchitis: acute and chronic. Each type has distinct causes, symptoms, and treatment approaches, making it essential for healthcare providers to differentiate between them for effective management.

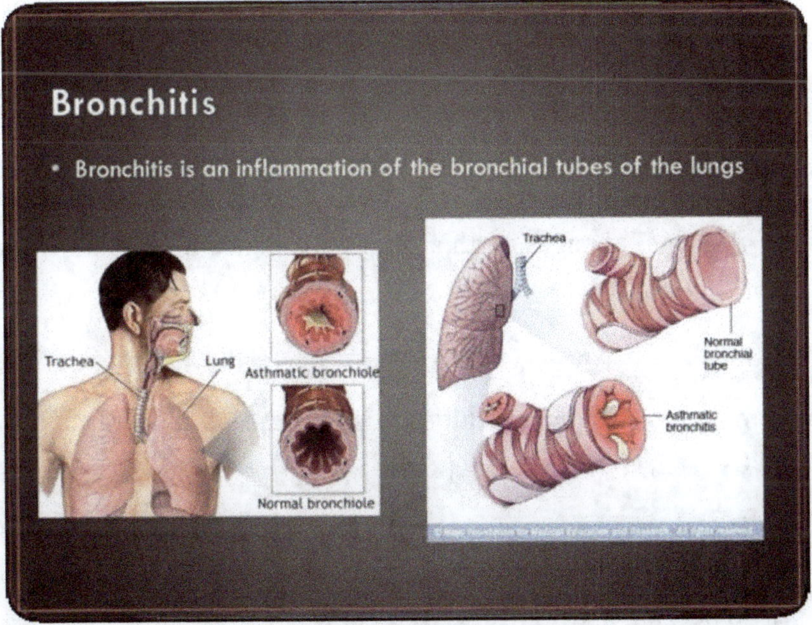

Acute Bronchitis

Acute bronchitis is a short-term condition that often follows a respiratory infection, such as the common cold or flu. It is typically caused by viral infections, though bacterial infections can also lead to acute bronchitis. The condition usually lasts for a few days to a few weeks and is characterized by a sudden onset of symptoms.

Causes and Risk Factors

The primary cause of acute bronchitis is a viral infection, accounting for approximately 90% of cases. Common viruses include influenza, rhinovirus, and respiratory syncytial virus (RSV). Bacterial infections, though less common, can also cause acute bronchitis. Common bacterial pathogens include Mycoplasma pneumoniae, Chlamydia pneumoniae, and Bordetella pertussis.

Risk factors for developing acute bronchitis include:

- Exposure to respiratory irritants such as tobacco smoke, dust, and chemical fumes
- Pre-existing respiratory conditions such as asthma or chronic obstructive pulmonary disease (COPD)
- A weakened immune system due to conditions like HIV/AIDS or certain medications
- Seasonal changes, with a higher incidence in fall and winter months

Symptoms

The symptoms of acute bronchitis typically develop suddenly and can include:

- Persistent cough, often producing mucus (sputum) that may be clear, yellow, or green
- Wheezing and shortness of breath
- Chest discomfort or tightness
- Low-grade fever and chills
- Fatigue and malaise

Chronic Bronchitis

Chronic bronchitis is a long-term condition that is a type of chronic obstructive pulmonary disease (COPD). It is characterized by a persistent cough that produces mucus for at least three months in two consecutive years. Chronic bronchitis is often caused by prolonged exposure to irritants that damage the bronchial tubes.

Causes and Risk Factors

The primary cause of chronic bronchitis is long-term exposure to irritants that inflame the bronchial tubes. The most common irritant is tobacco smoke, but other environmental pollutants and workplace exposures can also contribute to the condition.

Risk factors for chronic bronchitis include:

- Smoking: The most significant risk factor, with both active and passive smoking contributing to the development of chronic bronchitis
- Exposure to air pollution and occupational dusts and chemicals
- A history of frequent respiratory infections
- Genetic factors, including alpha-1 antitrypsin deficiency

Symptoms

The symptoms of chronic bronchitis are often more persistent and severe than those of acute bronchitis and can include:

- Chronic productive cough with sputum that is usually white or gray but may become discolored during infections
- Frequent respiratory infections
- Wheezing and shortness of breath, particularly during physical activity
- Fatigue and reduced ability to exercise
- Swelling in the ankles, feet, or legs due to fluid retention

Diagnosis

Diagnosing bronchitis involves a combination of clinical evaluation, patient history, and diagnostic tests. Healthcare providers typically begin with a thorough history and physical examination, focusing on the patient's symptoms, duration, and potential exposure to irritants or infectious agents.

Diagnostic Tests

Several tests can aid in diagnosing bronchitis and differentiating it from other respiratory conditions:

- Chest X-ray: Useful for ruling out pneumonia or other lung diseases
- Spirometry: Measures lung function and helps in diagnosing COPD, including chronic bronchitis
- Sputum culture: Identifies bacterial infections if suspected
- Blood tests: Check for signs of infection or inflammation
- Pulse oximetry: Measures oxygen levels in the blood to assess the severity of respiratory impairment

Treatment

The treatment approach for bronchitis varies based on whether the condition is acute or chronic.

Acute Bronchitis

Treatment for acute bronchitis focuses on relieving symptoms and may include:

- Rest and hydration: Ensuring adequate fluid intake and rest to support the immune system
- Cough suppressants: Medications such as dextromethorphan to reduce coughing
- Expectorants: Guaifenesin to help loosen and expel mucus

- Pain relievers: Over-the-counter medications like acetaminophen or ibuprofen to reduce fever and discomfort
- Bronchodilators: Inhaled medications to open airways in cases of wheezing or difficulty breathing

Chronic Bronchitis

Managing chronic bronchitis involves both pharmacological and non-pharmacological strategies:

- Smoking cessation: The most crucial step in managing and preventing progression
- Bronchodilators: Long-acting inhalers to open airways and reduce symptoms
- Corticosteroids: Inhaled or oral medications to reduce inflammation
- Oxygen therapy: For patients with severe COPD and low blood oxygen levels
- Pulmonary rehabilitation: A program of exercise, education, and support to improve lung function and quality of life
- Vaccinations: Annual flu vaccine and pneumococcal vaccine to prevent respiratory infections

Understanding the different types of bronchitis, their causes, symptoms, and treatment options is essential for healthcare providers. By accurately diagnosing and effectively managing both acute and chronic bronchitis, healthcare professionals can significantly improve patient outcomes and quality of life.

DISCUSSION QUESTIONS

- What are the primary differences between acute and chronic bronchitis in terms of etiology, symptoms, and duration?
- How does smoking contribute to the development of chronic bronchitis, and what are the implications for public health initiatives?

LESSON TWO: CLINICAL SIGNS AND SYMPTOMS OF BRONCHITIS

Bronchitis, whether acute or chronic, presents with a range of clinical signs and symptoms that healthcare providers must recognize to diagnose and manage the condition effectively. This lesson delves into the various clinical manifestations of bronchitis, highlighting the differences between acute and chronic forms, and providing insights into the nuances of patient presentation.

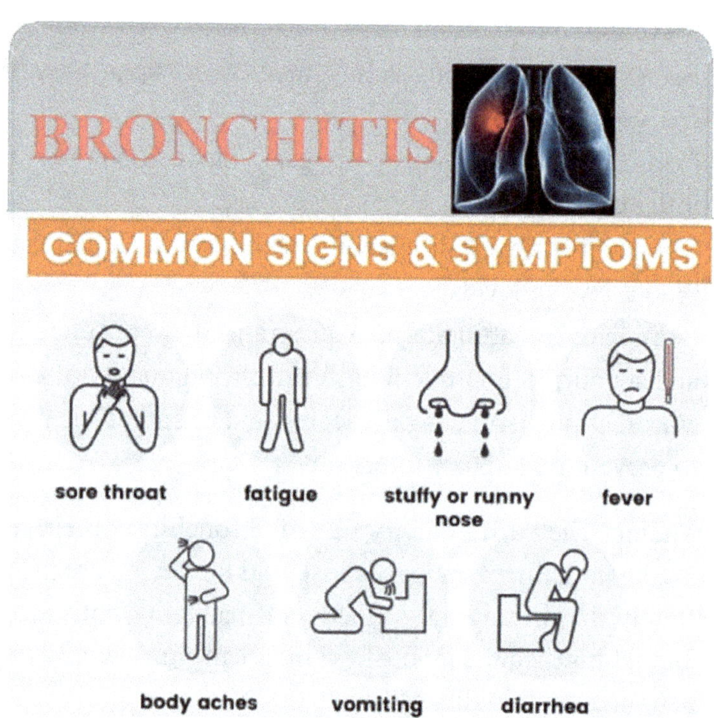

Acute Bronchitis

Acute bronchitis is characterized by the sudden onset of symptoms following a respiratory infection. The clinical signs and symptoms often overlap with those of other respiratory conditions, making a thorough patient history and examination crucial for accurate diagnosis.

Common Symptoms

- Cough: The hallmark symptom of acute bronchitis, typically starting as dry and becoming productive. The cough can persist for several weeks, even after other symptoms have resolved.
- Sputum Production: Mucus production is a common feature, with sputum that may be clear, yellow, or green, depending on the underlying infection.
- Wheezing: Inflammation of the bronchial tubes can cause wheezing, a high-pitched whistling sound during breathing, indicating airway obstruction.
- Shortness of Breath: Patients may experience difficulty breathing, especially during physical exertion, due to narrowed and inflamed airways.
- Chest Discomfort: A sensation of tightness or pain in the chest can occur, often exacerbated by coughing.
- Fever and Chills: Low-grade fever and chills are common, especially if the bronchitis is caused by a viral infection.
- Fatigue: Generalized tiredness and malaise are frequent complaints, likely due to the body's effort to fight off the infection.

Less Common Symptoms

- Hoarseness: Inflammation can extend to the vocal cords, causing a hoarse voice.
- Muscle Aches: Body aches and pains may accompany fever and malaise, particularly in viral infections.
- Sore Throat: The upper respiratory tract inflammation can lead to a sore throat, often preceding the onset of bronchitis symptoms.

Chronic Bronchitis

Chronic bronchitis, a form of chronic obstructive pulmonary disease (COPD), presents with more persistent and progressive symptoms. Recognizing the clinical signs of chronic bronchitis is essential for early intervention and management.

Common Symptoms

- Chronic Cough: A cough that lasts for at least three months in two consecutive years is the defining symptom of chronic bronchitis. The cough is typically productive, with mucus that is usually white or gray but may become discolored during infections.
- Sputum Production: Persistent mucus production is a key feature, often worse in the mornings and during infections.
- Shortness of Breath: Progressive difficulty breathing, especially during physical activity, is common. Over time, patients may experience dyspnea at rest.
- Wheezing: Similar to acute bronchitis, wheezing can occur due to airway obstruction.
- Frequent Respiratory Infections: Patients with chronic bronchitis are prone to recurrent respiratory infections, which can exacerbate symptoms.
- Fatigue: Chronic bronchitis can lead to significant fatigue, impacting the patient's ability to perform daily activities.

Advanced Symptoms

- Cyanosis: Bluish discoloration of the lips and skin due to low blood oxygen levels.
- Peripheral Edema: Swelling in the ankles, feet, or legs from fluid retention, indicating potential heart failure (cor pulmonale).

- Weight Loss: Unintentional weight loss and muscle wasting in severe cases, often due to increased energy expenditure from breathing efforts and reduced appetite.

Clinical Examination

A thorough clinical examination is essential for diagnosing bronchitis and assessing its severity. Key components of the examination include:

- Inspection: Observing the patient's overall appearance, breathing pattern, and any signs of respiratory distress or cyanosis.
- Palpation: Checking for tenderness over the chest wall and assessing for any lymphadenopathy.
- Percussion: Percussing the chest to detect any areas of dullness that might indicate consolidation or pleural effusion.
- Auscultation: Listening to the lungs with a stethoscope to identify abnormal breath sounds such as wheezing, crackles, or decreased breath sounds.

Diagnostic Criteria

Diagnosing bronchitis, particularly chronic bronchitis, requires meeting specific criteria based on patient history, clinical presentation, and diagnostic tests. For chronic bronchitis, the presence of a chronic productive cough for at least three months in two consecutive years is a key criterion.

Differential Diagnosis

Distinguishing bronchitis from other respiratory conditions is critical for appropriate management. Conditions to consider in the differential diagnosis include:

- Pneumonia: Typically presents with more severe symptoms, including high fever, chest pain, and significant findings on chest X-ray.
- Asthma: Characterized by recurrent episodes of wheezing, breathlessness, and cough, often with a known history of asthma or allergies.
- COPD: Includes chronic bronchitis and emphysema, with symptoms such as chronic cough, sputum production, and progressive dyspnea.
- Tuberculosis: Consider in patients with a chronic cough, weight loss, night sweats, and a history of exposure or travel to endemic areas.
- Lung Cancer: Persistent cough, hemoptysis, unexplained weight loss, and a history of smoking are red flags for malignancy.

Recognizing the clinical signs and symptoms of bronchitis, both acute and chronic, is essential for healthcare providers. By understanding the nuances of patient presentation and performing a thorough clinical examination, clinicians can accurately diagnose bronchitis and initiate appropriate management strategies to improve patient outcomes.

DISCUSSION QUESTIONS

- How can healthcare providers differentiate between the clinical signs of bronchitis and other respiratory conditions such as asthma or pneumonia?
- Discuss the importance of obtaining a thorough patient history and physical examination in the diagnosis of bronchitis.

MODULE TWO

LESSON ONE: PHYSIOLOGICAL MANIFESTATIONS OF BRONCHITIS

Bronchitis, characterized by the inflammation of the bronchial tubes, leads to various physiological changes in the respiratory system. Understanding these physiological manifestations is crucial for healthcare providers as it aids in diagnosis, treatment planning, and patient education. This lesson explores the physiological alterations that occur in both acute and chronic bronchitis.

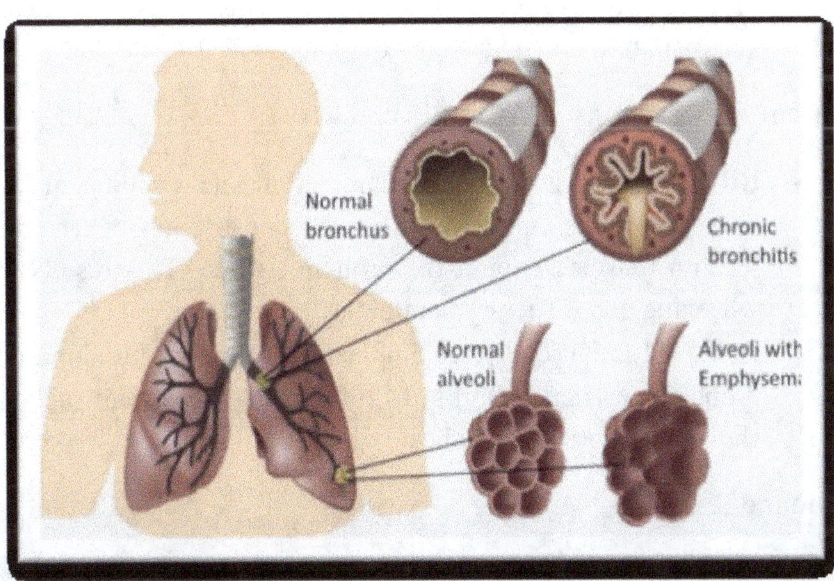

Acute Bronchitis

Acute bronchitis typically results from viral infections, although bacterial infections can also be a cause. The inflammation of the bronchial tubes in acute bronchitis triggers several physiological responses:

Inflammatory Response

- Mucosal Inflammation: The bronchial mucosa becomes inflamed and swollen, leading to narrowing of the airways. This inflammation is the body's response to infection or irritants.
- Increased Mucus Production: Goblet cells and submucosal glands in the bronchial walls produce excessive mucus in response to the inflammation. This mucus can be clear, yellow, or green, depending on the type of infection.
- Ciliary Dysfunction: The cilia, hair-like structures that help clear mucus and debris from the airways, become less effective due to the inflammation. This leads to mucus accumulation and persistent coughing.

Airway Obstruction

- Bronchoconstriction: The inflammation and swelling of the bronchial walls can lead to bronchoconstriction, where the smooth muscles around the bronchi tighten. This results in wheezing and difficulty breathing.
- Airflow Limitation: The combination of mucus buildup and bronchoconstriction limits airflow, causing symptoms such as shortness of breath and chest tightness.

Immune Response

- Immune Cell Infiltration: Inflammatory cells, including neutrophils, macrophages, and lymphocytes, infiltrate the bronchial walls to fight the infection. This immune response further contributes to the inflammation and mucus production.

Chronic Bronchitis

Chronic bronchitis, a type of chronic obstructive pulmonary disease (COPD), involves long-term inflammation and irritation of the bronchial tubes. This persistent inflammation leads to several physiological changes that contribute to the chronic and progressive nature of the disease:

Chronic Inflammation

- Thickening of the Bronchial Walls: Long-term inflammation causes the bronchial walls to thicken due to fibrosis and increased smooth muscle mass. This thickening narrows the airways and restricts airflow.
- Hyperplasia of Goblet Cells: The number of mucus-producing goblet cells increases, leading to excessive mucus production and chronic productive cough.
- Ciliary Dysfunction: Chronic inflammation damages the cilia, impairing their ability to clear mucus and debris from the airways.

Airway Remodeling

- Bronchial Wall Hypertrophy: The smooth muscles of the bronchial walls undergo hypertrophy (thickening), further narrowing the airways and contributing to airflow limitation.
- Mucus Gland Hypertrophy: The submucosal glands become enlarged, producing more mucus, which accumulates in the airways and causes obstruction.

Airflow Limitation

- Fixed Airflow Obstruction: Unlike the reversible bronchoconstriction seen in acute bronchitis, chronic bronchitis leads to fixed airflow obstruction due to structural changes in the bronchial walls.
- Reduced FEV1/FVC Ratio: Spirometry tests often show a reduced forced expiratory volume in one second (FEV1) to forced vital capacity (FVC) ratio, indicating obstructive lung disease.

Gas Exchange Impairment

- Ventilation-Perfusion Mismatch: Chronic bronchitis can lead to a mismatch between ventilation (airflow) and perfusion (blood flow) in the lungs, impairing gas exchange and leading to hypoxemia (low blood oxygen levels).
- Hypercapnia: In severe cases, the impaired gas exchange can cause hypercapnia (elevated carbon dioxide levels in the blood), leading to respiratory acidosis and further complications.

SYSTEMIC EFFECTS

Both acute and chronic bronchitis can have systemic effects beyond the respiratory system:

Acute Bronchitis

- Systemic Inflammatory Response: The body's immune response to infection can cause systemic symptoms such as fever, chills, and malaise.
- Impact on Other Organs: Severe infections can lead to complications such as pneumonia, which can further stress the cardiovascular and renal systems.

Chronic Bronchitis

- Chronic Inflammation: Persistent systemic inflammation in chronic bronchitis can contribute to comorbidities such as cardiovascular disease, metabolic syndrome, and osteoporosis.
- Pulmonary Hypertension: Chronic hypoxemia and inflammation can lead to increased pressure in the pulmonary arteries, resulting in pulmonary hypertension and right heart failure (cor pulmonale).

Understanding the physiological manifestations of bronchitis provides healthcare providers with critical insights into the mechanisms driving the symptoms and complications of the disease. By recognizing these physiological changes, clinicians can develop more effective treatment plans, improve patient education, and ultimately enhance patient outcomes. This knowledge is particularly vital for managing chronic bronchitis, where long-term strategies are required to address the ongoing inflammation and prevent disease progression.

DISCUSSION QUESTIONS

- What are the advantages and limitations of using spirometry in the diagnosis of bronchitis?
- How can imaging studies, such as chest X-rays, assist in distinguishing bronchitis from other pulmonary conditions?

LESSON TWO: RADIOGRAPHIC FEATURES: BRONCHITIS ON X-RAY

Radiographic imaging plays a crucial role in the diagnosis and management of bronchitis. While acute bronchitis often does not show specific findings on chest X-ray, chronic bronchitis and its complications can present with various radiographic features. This lesson explores the radiographic characteristics of bronchitis, with a focus on interpreting chest X-rays to aid in the diagnosis and differentiation from other respiratory conditions.

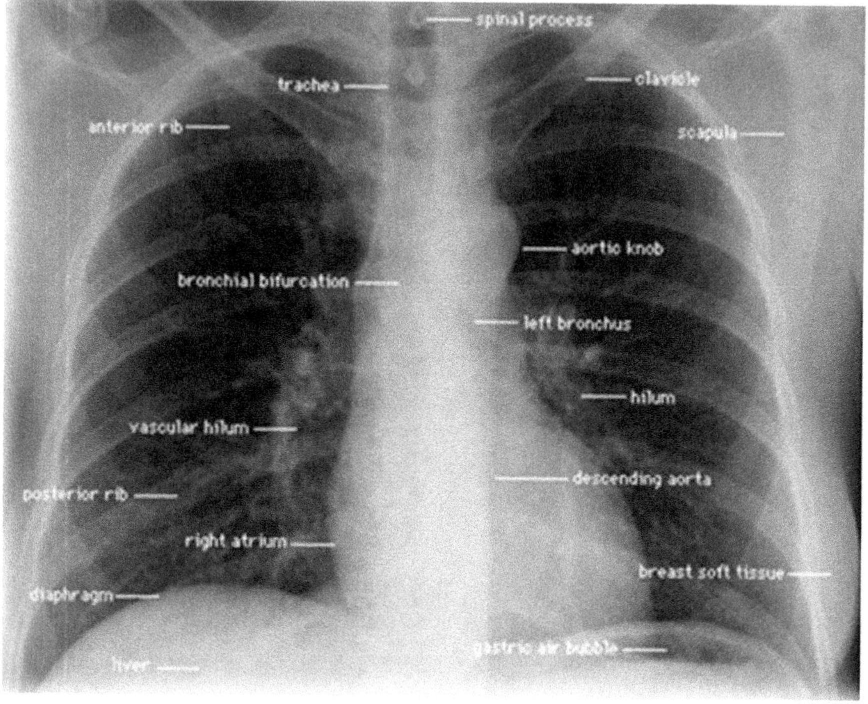

Acute Bronchitis

In acute bronchitis, chest X-rays are often performed to rule out pneumonia or other serious conditions rather than to confirm bronchitis, as acute bronchitis itself typically does not produce specific radiographic changes.

Common Radiographic Findings

- Normal Chest X-ray: Most patients with acute bronchitis will have a normal chest X-ray, as the inflammation is often confined to the bronchial mucosa and does not significantly affect the lung parenchyma.
- Increased Bronchial Wall Thickening: In some cases, mild bronchial wall thickening can be seen, indicating inflammation of the bronchial walls.
- Peribronchial Cuffing: This refers to the appearance of a thickened bronchial wall surrounded by fluid or mucus, visible as a ring-like shadow on the X-ray.

Differentiation from Pneumonia

- Lobar Consolidation: Pneumonia typically presents with lobar consolidation, which appears as a localized area of increased opacity in one or more lobes of the lung. This finding is not present in acute bronchitis.
- Air Bronchograms: The presence of air bronchograms (air-filled bronchi surrounded by alveolar consolidation) is a hallmark of pneumonia and is absent in uncomplicated acute bronchitis.

Chronic Bronchitis

Chronic bronchitis, as part of COPD, often presents with more pronounced and specific radiographic features compared to acute bronchitis. The chest X-ray findings in chronic bronchitis can provide valuable information for diagnosis and assessment of disease severity.

Common Radiographic Findings

- Increased Bronchovascular Markings: Chronic inflammation and fibrosis lead to prominent bronchovascular markings, especially in the lower lung fields. This reflects the thickening of the bronchial walls and increased vascularity.

- Hyperinflation: Patients with chronic bronchitis may show signs of lung hyperinflation, including a flattened diaphragm and increased retrosternal air space. This results from air trapping due to airway obstruction.
- Cardiomegaly: An enlarged heart silhouette can be seen in patients with advanced disease, particularly if there is associated cor pulmonale (right heart failure).
- Peribronchial Cuffing: Similar to acute bronchitis, peribronchial cuffing can be present due to chronic mucus accumulation and inflammation.

Differentiation from Emphysema

- Bullae and Blebs: Unlike chronic bronchitis, emphysema is characterized by the presence of bullae (large air-filled spaces) and blebs (small subpleural air-filled spaces) due to the destruction of alveolar walls.
- Reduced Vascular Markings: In emphysema, there is often a reduction in peripheral vascular markings due to the loss of alveolar capillaries, whereas chronic bronchitis shows increased bronchovascular markings.

Advanced Imaging Techniques

While chest X-rays are the primary imaging modality for initial assessment, advanced imaging techniques such as computed tomography (CT) scans can provide more detailed information about bronchial and parenchymal changes in chronic bronchitis.

Computed Tomography (CT) Scans

- High-Resolution CT (HRCT): HRCT is particularly useful for evaluating the extent of bronchial wall thickening, mucus plugging, and small airway disease in chronic bronchitis. It provides a more detailed view of the bronchial architecture and parenchymal changes.

- Air Trapping: HRCT can identify areas of air trapping, which are indicative of small airway obstruction and are not easily visible on standard chest X-rays.
- Emphysematous Changes: CT scans can also help differentiate chronic bronchitis from emphysema by clearly showing areas of parenchymal destruction and bullae formation.

Radiographic imaging is an essential tool in the evaluation of bronchitis, providing critical information for diagnosis and management. While chest X-rays are often normal in acute bronchitis, they are useful for ruling out other conditions such as pneumonia. In chronic bronchitis, chest X-rays and advanced imaging techniques like HRCT reveal specific features that aid in the assessment of disease severity and differentiation from other forms of COPD. By understanding and interpreting these radiographic findings, healthcare providers can make more accurate diagnoses and develop effective treatment plans for patients with bronchitis.

DISCUSSION QUESTIONS

- How should treatment plans for acute bronchitis differ from those for chronic bronchitis, and what factors should influence these decisions?
- Discuss the role of corticosteroids and bronchodilators in the management of chronic bronchitis and their potential side effects.

MODULE THREE

LESSON ONE: TREATMENT STRATEGIES FOR BRONCHITIS

Effective management of bronchitis involves a comprehensive approach that addresses the underlying causes, alleviates symptoms, and prevents complications. Treatment strategies differ based on whether the bronchitis is acute or chronic. This lesson outlines evidence-based treatment options for both forms of bronchitis, including pharmacological and non-pharmacological interventions.

Bronchitis treatment

Indications for hospitalization

- Severe course of bacterial bronchitis, manifested signs of intoxication
- Complicated bronchitis – with manifested mucus retention, impaired bronchial patency, atelectasis formation etc.
- Bronchiolitis (in children of less than 1 y.o. because of threatening of emergency conditions)
- Severe types of Obstructive bronchitis (OB) – especially resistant for treatment in ambulatory conditions
- Lingering and recurrent bronchitis (for diagnostic and treatment)
- Chronic forms of disease (for treatment and full examining)
- Bronchitis on the ground of another somatic severe diseases (CNS, anomalies and malformations of organs chronic disorders
- Social reasons

Acute Bronchitis

Acute bronchitis is typically self-limiting and often resolves without specific medical treatment. However, symptomatic relief and addressing the underlying cause are crucial to patient comfort and recovery.

Symptomatic Treatment

- Rest and Hydration: Adequate rest and fluid intake are fundamental to help the body recover and to thin mucus, making it easier to expel.
- Antipyretics and Analgesics: Over-the-counter medications such as acetaminophen or ibuprofen can reduce fever, relieve pain, and decrease inflammation.
- Cough Suppressants: Medications like dextromethorphan may be used to suppress a bothersome cough, but they should be used sparingly as coughing helps clear mucus.
- Expectorants: Guaifenesin can help thin mucus and make it easier to cough up, providing relief from chest congestion.

Antibiotic Use

- When Indicated: Antibiotics are generally not recommended for acute bronchitis since most cases are viral. However, they may be prescribed if there is a high suspicion of bacterial infection or if the patient has a history of chronic respiratory conditions that could be exacerbated by bacterial infection.
- Common Choices: When antibiotics are necessary, options include amoxicillin, doxycycline, or macrolides like azithromycin.

Antiviral Medications

- Indications: Antiviral medications may be considered if influenza is the underlying cause of bronchitis and the patient is at high risk for complications.
- Common Antivirals: Oseltamivir or zanamivir are commonly used to treat influenza.

Chronic Bronchitis

Chronic bronchitis, a form of COPD, requires a long-term management plan to control symptoms, slow disease progression, and prevent exacerbations.

Smoking Cessation

- Primary Intervention: Smoking cessation is the single most effective intervention for patients with chronic bronchitis. It halts further damage to the airways and can significantly improve symptoms and lung function.
- Support Programs: Nicotine replacement therapy, medications such as varenicline or bupropion, and behavioral therapy can aid in quitting smoking.

Pharmacological Treatments

- Bronchodilators:
- Short-Acting Beta Agonists (SABAs): Medications like albuterol provide quick relief from bronchoconstriction and are used on an as-needed basis.
- Long-Acting Beta Agonists (LABAs): Salmeterol or formoterol are used for maintenance therapy to help keep airways open.
- Anticholinergics: Ipratropium (short-acting) or tiotropium (long-acting) help reduce mucus production and relax airway muscles.
- Inhaled Corticosteroids (ICS): Fluticasone or budesonide can reduce inflammation in the airways, though they are typically reserved for patients with frequent exacerbations.
- Combination Inhalers: LABA/ICS combinations (e.g., fluticasone/salmeterol) provide both bronchodilation and anti-inflammatory effects.

- Phosphodiesterase-4 Inhibitors: Roflumilast can be used to reduce exacerbations in severe COPD with chronic bronchitis.
- Mucolytics: Medications like carbocisteine may be used to thin mucus, making it easier to clear.

Non-Pharmacological Treatments

- Pulmonary Rehabilitation: A comprehensive program that includes exercise training, education, and behavior modification designed to improve the physical and emotional condition of people with chronic respiratory disease.
- Oxygen Therapy: Long-term oxygen therapy can be beneficial for patients with chronic hypoxemia, improving quality of life and survival.
- Nutritional Support: Maintaining proper nutrition is crucial as chronic bronchitis can lead to weight loss and muscle wasting.

Managing Exacerbations

- Early Intervention: Prompt recognition and treatment of exacerbations are vital. This may involve increasing the dose or frequency of bronchodilators, using oral corticosteroids, and administering antibiotics if a bacterial infection is suspected.
- Hospitalization: Severe exacerbations may require hospitalization for intensive treatment, including oxygen therapy, intravenous medications, and possibly mechanical ventilation.

Preventive Measures

- Vaccinations: Annual influenza vaccination and pneumococcal vaccination can prevent infections that may exacerbate bronchitis.

- Avoiding Irritants: Reducing exposure to air pollutants, dust, and occupational irritants can help manage symptoms and prevent exacerbations.
- Regular Monitoring: Routine follow-ups with healthcare providers to monitor lung function and adjust treatment plans as needed.

Effective management of bronchitis, particularly chronic bronchitis, requires a multifaceted approach that includes lifestyle modifications, pharmacological treatments, and preventive measures. By addressing both the symptoms and underlying causes of bronchitis, healthcare providers can significantly improve patient outcomes and quality of life. Education on the importance of smoking cessation, adherence to treatment plans, and regular monitoring is essential for long-term disease management.

DISCUSSION QUESTION

- What are the key components of effective patient education for individuals diagnosed with bronchitis?
- How can healthcare providers encourage patient adherence to self-management plans, and what are some common barriers to adherence?

LEESON TWO: MEDICATIONS FOR BRONCHITIS

Pharmacotherapy is a cornerstone in the management of bronchitis, particularly chronic bronchitis. This lesson provides an in-depth look at the various medications used to treat bronchitis, including their mechanisms of action, indications, dosages, and potential side effects. Understanding these medications is crucial for healthcare providers to optimize treatment plans and improve patient outcomes.

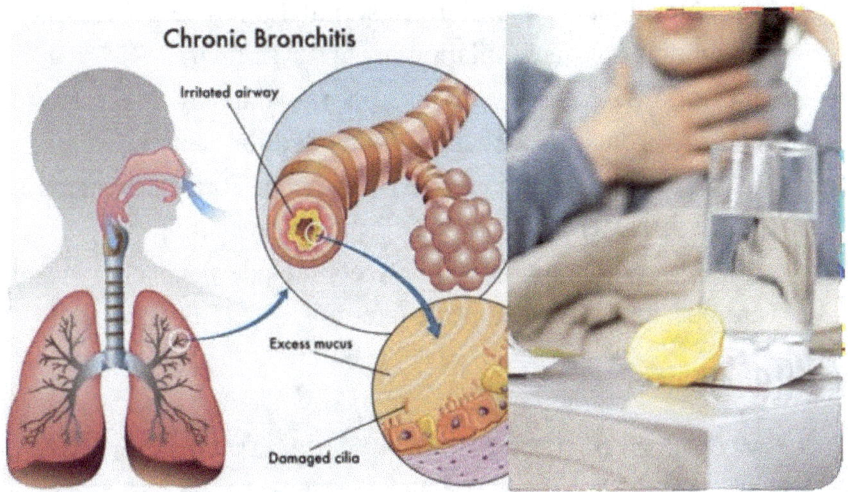

Bronchodilators

Bronchodilators are medications that relax the muscles around the airways, making it easier to breathe. They are commonly used in both acute and chronic bronchitis to relieve symptoms of bronchoconstriction.

Short-Acting Beta Agonists (SABAs)

- Mechanism of Action: SABAs, such as albuterol, stimulate beta-2 adrenergic receptors in the lungs, causing the bronchial muscles to relax and dilate the airways.
- Indications: SABAs are used for quick relief of acute bronchospasm and are often referred to as "rescue" inhalers.

- Dosage: The typical dosage for albuterol is 2.5 mg via nebulizer or 90-180 mcg via metered-dose inhaler (MDI) every 4-6 hours as needed.
- Side Effects: Common side effects include tremors, palpitations, tachycardia, and nervousness.

Long-Acting Beta Agonists (LABAs)

- Mechanism of Action: LABAs, such as salmeterol and formoterol, provide prolonged stimulation of beta-2 receptors, maintaining bronchodilation for up to 12 hours.
- Indications: LABAs are used for maintenance therapy in chronic bronchitis and are not intended for acute relief.
- Dosage: Salmeterol is typically dosed at 50 mcg twice daily, while formoterol is dosed at 12 mcg twice daily.
- Side Effects: Potential side effects include headache, muscle cramps, and increased heart rate.

Anticholinergics

- Mechanism of Action: Anticholinergics, such as ipratropium and tiotropium, block the action of acetylcholine on muscarinic receptors, reducing bronchoconstriction and mucus production.
- Indications: These medications are used for both acute and maintenance therapy in bronchitis.
- Dosage: Ipratropium is usually dosed at 500 mcg via nebulizer or 18 mcg via MDI four times daily. Tiotropium is dosed at 18 mcg once daily.
- Side Effects: Common side effects include dry mouth, constipation, and urinary retention.

Inhaled Corticosteroids (ICS)

Inhaled corticosteroids reduce inflammation in the airways, helping to control symptoms and prevent exacerbations in chronic bronchitis.

- Mechanism of Action: ICS, such as fluticasone and budesonide, inhibit inflammatory mediators and reduce bronchial hyperresponsiveness.
- Indications: ICS are used in patients with chronic bronchitis who have frequent exacerbations or severe symptoms.
- Dosage: Fluticasone is typically dosed at 100-250 mcg twice daily, while budesonide is dosed at 200-400 mcg twice daily.
- Side Effects: Potential side effects include oral thrush, hoarseness, and increased risk of pneumonia.

Combination Inhalers

Combination inhalers contain both a LABA and an ICS, providing the benefits of both bronchodilation and anti-inflammatory effects.

- Common Combinations: Fluticasone/salmeterol (Advair) and budesonide/formoterol (Symbicort) are common combinations used in chronic bronchitis.
- Dosage: Advair is typically dosed at 100/50 mcg to 500/50 mcg twice daily, while Symbicort is dosed at 80/4.5 mcg to 160/4.5 mcg twice daily.
- Side Effects: Combination inhalers share side effects of both LABAs and ICS, including the risk of oral thrush and cardiovascular effects.

Phosphodiesterase-4 Inhibitors

Phosphodiesterase-4 inhibitors, such as roflumilast, are used to reduce inflammation and prevent exacerbations in severe chronic bronchitis.

- Mechanism of Action: Roflumilast inhibits the enzyme phosphodiesterase-4, leading to reduced inflammation and mucus production in the airways.

- Indications: Roflumilast is indicated for patients with severe COPD and chronic bronchitis who have frequent exacerbations.
- Dosage: The typical dosage is 500 mcg orally once daily.
- Side Effects: Common side effects include diarrhea, weight loss, and nausea.

Mucolytics

Mucolytics help thin and loosen mucus, making it easier to clear from the airways.

- Mechanism of Action: Mucolytics, such as carbocisteine, reduce the viscosity of mucus by breaking down the bonds within the mucus structure.
- Indications: Mucolytics are used in chronic bronchitis to manage persistent mucus production.
- Dosage: Carbocisteine is typically dosed at 375 mg to 750 mg three times daily.
- Side Effects: Potential side effects include gastrointestinal discomfort and skin rash.

Antibiotics and Antivirals

While antibiotics and antivirals are not routinely used in all cases of bronchitis, they are important in certain situations.

Antibiotics

- Indications: Antibiotics are prescribed when bacterial infection is suspected or in patients with chronic bronchitis experiencing an acute exacerbation.
- Common Choices: Amoxicillin, doxycycline, and macrolides (e.g., azithromycin) are commonly used antibiotics.
- Dosage: Amoxicillin is typically dosed at 500 mg to 875 mg twice daily for 7-10 days, doxycycline at 100 mg twice daily,

and azithromycin as a 5-day course with 500 mg on day 1 and 250 mg on days 2-5.

- Side Effects: Side effects may include gastrointestinal upset, allergic reactions, and antibiotic resistance.

Antivirals

- Indications: Antiviral medications are considered for bronchitis caused by influenza, especially in high-risk patients.
- Common Antivirals: Oseltamivir (Tamiflu) and zanamivir (Relenza) are commonly used to treat influenza.
- Dosage: Oseltamivir is dosed at 75 mg twice daily for 5 days, while zanamivir is inhaled at 10 mg twice daily for 5 days.
- Side Effects: Side effects can include nausea, vomiting, and respiratory discomfort.

Understanding the various medications available for treating bronchitis, particularly chronic bronchitis, is essential for healthcare providers. By selecting appropriate pharmacological therapies based on the patient's specific condition and symptoms, clinicians can effectively manage bronchitis, improve patient outcomes, and enhance the quality of life for those suffering from this respiratory condition. Ongoing education and patient adherence to prescribed treatments are vital components of successful bronchitis management.

DISCUSSION QUESTION

- How does the management of bronchitis in children differ from that in adults, and what unique challenges do pediatric patients present?
- Discuss the considerations for managing bronchitis in elderly patients, particularly those with multiple comorbidities.

MODULE FOUR

LESSON ONE: PATIENT EDUCATION AND SELF-MANAGEMENT

Effective management of bronchitis extends beyond medical treatments to include comprehensive patient education and self-management strategies. Educating patients about their condition, medications, lifestyle modifications, and preventive measures empowers them to take an active role in their healthcare. This lesson provides guidelines for healthcare providers on how to educate and support patients with bronchitis.

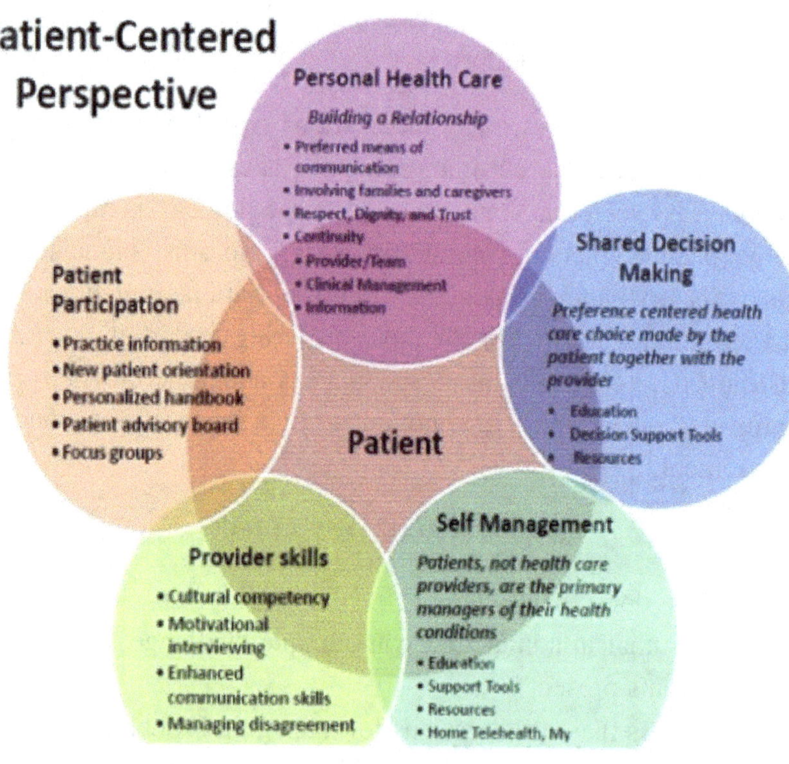

Understanding Bronchitis

Disease Overview

- Acute Bronchitis: Explain that acute bronchitis is a short-term inflammation of the bronchial tubes, usually caused by viral infections, and typically resolves on its own within a few weeks.
- Chronic Bronchitis: Discuss that chronic bronchitis is a long-term condition characterized by persistent cough and mucus production, often associated with smoking and part of COPD.

Symptoms and Complications

- Common Symptoms: Educate patients about the typical symptoms of bronchitis, such as cough, mucus production, shortness of breath, wheezing, and chest discomfort.
- Potential Complications: Highlight the importance of recognizing complications, such as pneumonia, and the need for prompt medical attention if symptoms worsen or new symptoms develop.

Medication Adherence

Importance of Adherence

- Explain Benefits: Emphasize the importance of taking medications as prescribed to control symptoms, prevent exacerbations, and improve overall health.
- Discuss Consequences: Discuss the potential consequences of non-adherence, including worsening symptoms, increased risk of complications, and reduced quality of life.

Strategies for Adherence

- Simplify Regimen: Work with patients to simplify medication regimens when possible, such as using combination inhalers or long-acting medications.

- Use Reminders: Encourage the use of reminders, such as alarms, pill organizers, or smartphone apps, to help patients remember to take their medications.
- Address Barriers: Identify and address any barriers to adherence, such as side effects, cost, or difficulty using inhalers, and provide solutions or alternatives.

Lifestyle Modifications

Smoking Cessation

- Primary Goal: Stress the critical importance of quitting smoking to prevent further lung damage and improve symptoms.
- Support Options: Provide information on smoking cessation programs, medications, and resources to support patients in their efforts to quit.

Healthy Diet and Nutrition

- Balanced Diet: Encourage a balanced diet rich in fruits, vegetables, whole grains, and lean proteins to support overall health and immune function.
- Hydration: Advise patients to stay well-hydrated to help thin mucus and ease expectoration.

Physical Activity

- Exercise Benefits: Explain the benefits of regular physical activity, including improved respiratory function, increased energy, and enhanced mood.
- Activity Recommendations: Suggest suitable exercises, such as walking, swimming, or pulmonary rehabilitation programs, tailored to the patient's abilities and limitations.

Preventive Measures

Vaccinations

- Influenza Vaccine: Recommend annual influenza vaccination to prevent respiratory infections that can exacerbate bronchitis.
- Pneumococcal Vaccine: Advise pneumococcal vaccination for eligible patients to reduce the risk of bacterial pneumonia.

Avoiding Triggers

- Environmental Control: Educate patients on avoiding respiratory irritants, such as air pollution, dust, fumes, and strong odors.
- Infection Prevention: Encourage good hygiene practices, such as regular handwashing and avoiding close contact with sick individuals, to prevent respiratory infections.

Monitoring and Follow-Up

Regular Check-Ups

- Scheduled Visits: Stress the importance of regular follow-up appointments to monitor lung function, assess symptoms, and adjust treatment plans as needed.
- Self-Monitoring: Teach patients how to monitor their symptoms and recognize signs of exacerbations or complications.

Action Plan for Exacerbations

- Early Intervention: Provide patients with a clear action plan for managing exacerbations, including when to increase medication doses, start rescue medications, and seek medical attention.

- Emergency Contacts: Ensure patients know who to contact in case of severe symptoms or emergencies.

Psychological Support

Emotional Well-Being

- Mental Health: Address the psychological impact of chronic illness and provide resources for mental health support, such as counseling or support groups.
- Stress Management: Teach stress management techniques, such as relaxation exercises, mindfulness, and breathing exercises, to help patients cope with their condition.

Patient education and self-management are integral components of effective bronchitis care. By providing patients with the knowledge, skills, and resources they need to manage their condition, healthcare providers can help improve adherence, reduce exacerbations, and enhance overall quality of life. Empowered patients are better equipped to take an active role in their healthcare, leading to better outcomes and greater satisfaction with their treatment.

DISCUSSION QUESTIONS

- What evidence exists to support the use of herbal remedies in the management of bronchitis, and how should they be integrated into conventional treatment plans?
- How can practices such as yoga and acupuncture be used to complement traditional medical treatments for bronchitis, and what are the potential benefits?

LESSON TWO: DIRECTIONS AND RESEARCH IN BRONCHITIS MANAGEMENT

Advancements in the understanding and treatment of bronchitis continue to evolve, driven by ongoing research and innovation. This lesson explores the future directions in bronchitis management, including emerging therapies, new diagnostic tools, and the potential impact of precision medicine. Healthcare providers must stay informed about these developments to offer the best possible care to their patients.

EMERGING THERAPIES

Novel Anti-Inflammatory Agents

- Targeted Therapies: Research is focused on developing new anti-inflammatory agents that specifically target the inflammatory pathways involved in bronchitis, potentially reducing side effects and improving efficacy.
- Biologic Therapies: Biologics, such as monoclonal antibodies, are being investigated for their potential to modulate the immune response and reduce inflammation in chronic bronchitis.

Regenerative Medicine

- Stem Cell Therapy: Stem cell therapy holds promise for repairing damaged lung tissue and restoring normal lung function in patients with chronic bronchitis. Clinical trials are underway to evaluate the safety and efficacy of these treatments.
- Gene Therapy: Advances in gene therapy offer the potential to correct genetic defects and modify the disease course in bronchitis, particularly in cases with a genetic component.

New Diagnostic Tools

Biomarkers

- Identification of Biomarkers: Research is focused on identifying biomarkers that can provide early and accurate diagnosis of bronchitis, predict disease progression, and guide treatment decisions.
- Non-Invasive Testing: Development of non-invasive tests, such as breath analysis and blood tests, to detect biomarkers of bronchitis is a key area of research.

Imaging Techniques

- Advanced Imaging: Innovations in imaging technology, such as high-resolution computed tomography (HRCT) and magnetic resonance imaging (MRI), are improving the ability to detect and monitor bronchial inflammation and structural changes.
- Functional Imaging: Functional imaging techniques, such as positron emission tomography (PET) scans, are being explored to assess lung function and inflammation in real-time.

Precision Medicine

Personalized Treatment Plans

- Genetic Profiling: Genetic profiling can help identify patients who are likely to benefit from specific treatments, allowing for more personalized and effective management of bronchitis.
- Tailored Therapies: Precision medicine aims to tailor therapies based on individual patient characteristics, such as genetic makeup, environmental exposures, and disease phenotype.

Preventive Strategies

Vaccination Development

- New Vaccines: Research is ongoing to develop new vaccines that protect against a broader range of respiratory pathogens, potentially reducing the incidence of bronchitis and its exacerbations.
- Boosters and Updates: Enhancing existing vaccines with booster doses or updated formulations to address emerging

strains of viruses and bacteria is a focus of preventive strategies.

Lifestyle Interventions

- Digital Health Tools: The use of digital health tools, such as mobile apps and wearable devices, to monitor symptoms, track medication adherence, and provide real-time feedback is an emerging trend in bronchitis management.
- Telehealth Services: Telehealth services offer convenient access to healthcare providers, enabling timely interventions and continuous monitoring of patients with bronchitis.

Policy and Public Health Initiatives

Air Quality Improvement

- Environmental Regulations: Strengthening environmental regulations to reduce air pollution and exposure to respiratory irritants is crucial for preventing bronchitis and other respiratory conditions.
- Public Health Campaigns: Public health campaigns aimed at raising awareness about the impact of air quality on respiratory health and promoting measures to reduce exposure are essential.

Smoking Cessation Programs

- Enhanced Support: Expanding access to smoking cessation programs, including counseling, medications, and support groups, is vital for reducing the incidence of chronic bronchitis.
- Youth Prevention: Targeting youth with prevention programs to reduce the initiation of smoking and other tobacco use is a key strategy for long-term impact.

The future of bronchitis management is promising, with advancements in therapies, diagnostics, and personalized medicine paving the way for improved patient outcomes. Healthcare providers must stay abreast of these developments to offer cutting-edge care and educate patients about new treatment options. By embracing innovation and focusing on prevention, the medical community can make significant strides in reducing the burden of bronchitis and enhancing the quality of life for those affected by this condition.

DISCUSSION QUESTION

- What strategies can healthcare providers implement to prevent the onset of chronic bronchitis in at-risk populations?
- Discuss the role of lifestyle modifications, such as smoking cessation and environmental control, in the long-term management of bronchitis.

MODULE FIVE

LESSON ONE: SPECIAL POPULATIONS IN BRONCHITIS MANAGEMENT

Bronchitis can affect various populations differently, requiring tailored approaches to management. This lesson focuses on special populations, including children, the elderly, and individuals with comorbidities, detailing specific considerations and strategies for each group.

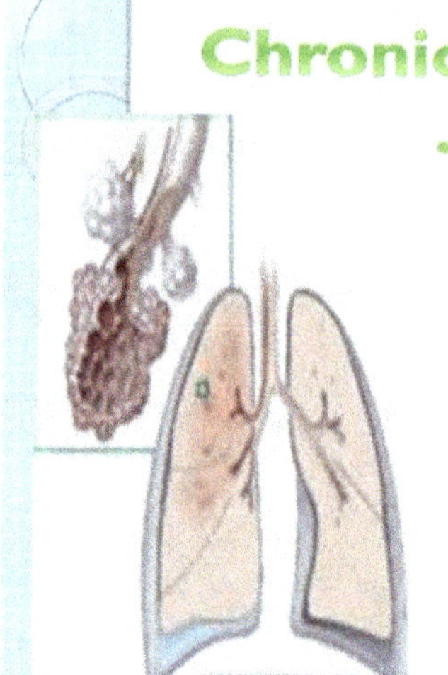

Bronchitis in Children

Acute Bronchitis

- Common Causes: Acute bronchitis in children is often caused by viral infections, such as respiratory syncytial virus (RSV) and influenza.

- Symptoms: Children may present with cough, wheezing, low-grade fever, and increased mucus production.
- Management: Emphasis is on supportive care, including hydration, rest, and antipyretics for fever. Antibiotics are generally not indicated unless there is a secondary bacterial infection.
- Prevention: Vaccination against influenza and other respiratory pathogens, good hand hygiene, and avoiding exposure to smoke and pollutants are key preventive measures.

Chronic Bronchitis

- Less Common: Chronic bronchitis is less common in children but can occur in those with underlying conditions such as cystic fibrosis or primary ciliary dyskinesia.
- Management: Treatment focuses on managing the underlying condition, using bronchodilators and anti-inflammatory medications as needed, and ensuring regular follow-up with pediatric specialists.

Bronchitis in the Elderly

Increased Risk

- Vulnerability: The elderly are more susceptible to bronchitis due to age-related changes in the immune system and the presence of comorbidities such as COPD and heart disease.
- Symptoms: Symptoms may be more severe and prolonged, including persistent cough, wheezing, dyspnea, and fatigue.
- Complications: There is a higher risk of complications, such as pneumonia and exacerbations of existing chronic conditions.

Management

- Medications: Careful selection of medications is necessary to avoid adverse effects and interactions with other drugs. Lower doses and close monitoring may be required.
- Supportive Care: Ensuring adequate nutrition, hydration, and respiratory support is crucial. Pulmonary rehabilitation programs can help improve lung function and physical endurance.
- Vaccination: Regular vaccination for influenza and pneumococcus is strongly recommended to prevent respiratory infections.

Bronchitis in Individuals with Comorbidities

Asthma

- Overlap: Patients with both asthma and bronchitis, particularly chronic bronchitis, require integrated management to control inflammation and bronchospasm.
- Medications: Inhaled corticosteroids, bronchodilators, and leukotriene modifiers are commonly used. Monitoring and adjusting treatment based on symptom control and lung function tests are essential.

Heart Disease

- Impact: Bronchitis can exacerbate heart disease by increasing the workload on the heart and reducing oxygenation.
- Management: Close coordination between respiratory and cardiology specialists is necessary. Medications to control heart failure symptoms and improve lung function should be optimized.

Diabetes

- Risk of Infection: Diabetic patients are at higher risk for infections, including bronchitis, due to compromised immune function.
- Management: Good glycemic control is essential to reduce infection risk. Antibiotics may be required for bacterial infections, and monitoring for drug interactions is important.

Psychological and Social Considerations

Anxiety and Depression

- Mental Health: Chronic respiratory symptoms can contribute to anxiety and depression, impacting overall quality of life.
- Support: Providing psychological support, counseling, and medications for mental health conditions can improve patient outcomes.

Socioeconomic Factors

- Access to Care: Socioeconomic factors can affect access to healthcare, adherence to treatment, and overall disease management.
- Interventions: Addressing barriers to care, such as providing transportation assistance, financial support for medications, and community health programs, can help improve management in underserved populations.

Managing bronchitis in special populations requires a nuanced approach that considers the unique challenges and needs of each group. By tailoring treatment strategies and providing comprehensive support, healthcare providers can enhance care and improve outcomes for children, the elderly, and individuals with comorbidities. Continuous education and advocacy for these populations are essential for effective bronchitis management.

- What are some of the latest findings in bronchitis research, and how might they impact clinical practice in the near future?
- Discuss the potential for precision medicine in the treatment of bronchitis, and what challenges might arise in its implementation.

MODULE SIX

LESSON ONE: INTEGRATIVE AND COMPLEMENTARY THERAPIES FOR BRONCHITIS

Integrative and complementary therapies can play a supportive role in the management of bronchitis, particularly for symptom relief and overall well-being. This lesson explores various integrative approaches, including herbal remedies, acupuncture, yoga, and dietary supplements, providing evidence-based information on their use and potential benefits.

Bronchitis

- Inflammation of the bronchial lining and excessive mucous production.
- Persistent cough, coughing up phlegm (mucous), which is often discoloured.
- Discomfort when breathing.
  - Acute Bronchitis – bacterial / viral infection (e.g., bad cold)
  - Chronic Bronchitis – allergens, airborne pollutants

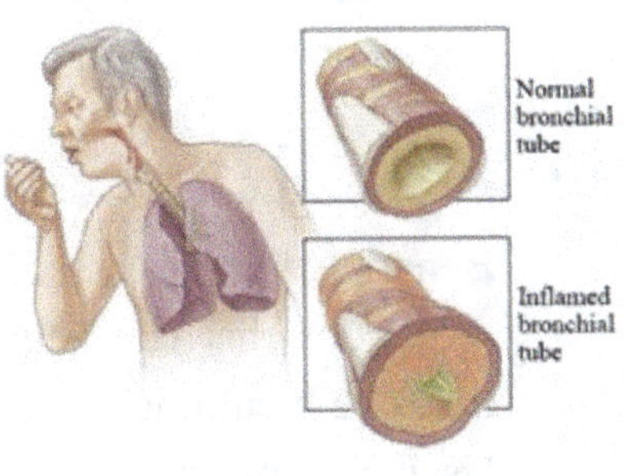

Herbal Remedies

Echinacea

- Benefits: Echinacea is believed to boost the immune system and may help reduce the severity and duration of acute bronchitis symptoms.

- Usage: Typically taken as a tea, tincture, or capsule. Standardized extracts are preferred to ensure consistency and potency.
- Safety: Generally safe when used short-term. Possible side effects include gastrointestinal upset and allergic reactions, particularly in individuals with allergies to plants in the daisy family.

Licorice Root

- Benefits: Licorice root has anti-inflammatory and expectorant properties, which can help soothe irritated airways and reduce mucus production.
- Usage: Available as a tea, extract, or lozenge. It is often used in traditional medicine for respiratory conditions.
- Safety: Long-term use is not recommended due to potential side effects, such as high blood pressure, potassium imbalance, and interactions with medications.

Ginger

- Benefits: Ginger has anti-inflammatory and bronchodilator properties that can help reduce bronchial inflammation and improve breathing.
- Usage: Consumed as a tea, fresh root, or supplement. It is commonly used in traditional and alternative medicine.
- Safety: Generally safe, with possible mild side effects like heartburn and gastrointestinal discomfort.

Acupuncture

Mechanism

- Theory: Acupuncture, a practice rooted in Traditional Chinese Medicine (TCM), involves inserting thin needles into specific points on the body to restore balance and improve health.

- Benefits: Acupuncture may help reduce symptoms of bronchitis by promoting relaxation, reducing inflammation, and improving respiratory function.

Evidence

- Studies: Some clinical trials suggest that acupuncture can reduce the frequency and severity of respiratory symptoms, though more research is needed to establish definitive efficacy.
- Safety: Generally considered safe when performed by a licensed practitioner. Potential side effects include minor bleeding, bruising, and soreness at needle sites.

Yoga and Breathing Exercises

Yoga

- Benefits: Yoga can improve respiratory function, enhance physical strength and flexibility, reduce stress, and promote overall well-being.
- Practices: Specific yoga poses (asanas) and breathing exercises (pranayama) are beneficial for respiratory health. Examples include the cobra pose, seated forward bend, and alternate nostril breathing.

Breathing Exercises

- Techniques: Breathing exercises, such as diaphragmatic breathing, pursed-lip breathing, and the Buteyko method, can help improve lung capacity, reduce shortness of breath, and enhance relaxation.
- Implementation: Regular practice of these techniques can aid in managing chronic bronchitis symptoms and improving overall respiratory health.

Dietary Supplements

Vitamin C

- Benefits: Vitamin C is an antioxidant that supports the immune system and may help reduce the duration and severity of respiratory infections.
- Dosage: Recommended daily intake varies, with higher doses often used during acute illness. Common supplementation ranges from 500 mg to 2000 mg per day.
- Safety: Generally safe, but high doses can cause gastrointestinal upset and, rarely, kidney stones.

Zinc

- Benefits: Zinc plays a vital role in immune function and may help reduce the duration of acute bronchitis symptoms.
- Dosage: Typical supplementation ranges from 15 mg to 30 mg per day. Lozenges are often used during acute respiratory infections.
- Safety: Long-term use of high doses can lead to zinc toxicity and interfere with copper absorption.

Aromatherapy

Essential Oils

- Benefits: Essential oils, such as eucalyptus, peppermint, and tea tree oil, have antimicrobial and anti-inflammatory properties that can help alleviate bronchitis symptoms.
- Usage: Oils can be used in diffusers, steam inhalation, or diluted in carrier oils for topical application.
- Safety: Essential oils should be used with caution, particularly in children and those with allergies. Proper dilution and avoiding ingestion are essential to prevent adverse effects.

Integrative and complementary therapies can offer valuable support in the management of bronchitis, enhancing symptom relief and overall quality of life. While these therapies should not replace conventional medical treatments, they can be used in conjunction with standard care to provide a holistic approach to bronchitis management. Healthcare providers should stay informed about these options and guide patients in safely incorporating them into their treatment plans.

<h3 style="text-align:center">DISCUSSION QUESTION</h3>

- How can case studies be used to enhance the understanding of bronchitis management among healthcare providers?
- Discuss a clinical scenario where a patient with bronchitis presents with atypical symptoms. How would you approach the diagnosis and treatment?

MODULE SEVEN

LESSON ONE: THE ROLE OF TECHNOLOGY IN BRONCHITIS MANAGEMENT

In recent years, technological advancements have significantly transformed healthcare, including the management of bronchitis. This lesson explores the various technologies that are enhancing the diagnosis, treatment, and monitoring of bronchitis, emphasizing the importance of staying abreast of these developments to provide optimal patient care.

Telemedicine

Remote Consultations

- Accessibility: Telemedicine enables patients to consult with healthcare providers remotely, improving access to care, especially for those in rural or underserved areas.

- Convenience: Patients can receive medical advice, prescription refills, and follow-up care without the need to travel, reducing the burden on both patients and the healthcare system.
- Continuity of Care: Telemedicine ensures continuity of care for chronic bronchitis patients by allowing regular monitoring and timely intervention for exacerbations.

Virtual Pulmonary Rehabilitation

- Programs: Virtual pulmonary rehabilitation programs offer structured exercise and education sessions delivered through online platforms, making them accessible to a broader range of patients.
- Benefits: These programs can improve lung function, enhance physical fitness, and provide ongoing support and education, helping patients manage their condition more effectively.

Wearable Devices

Monitoring Respiratory Function

- Devices: Wearable devices, such as smartwatches and fitness trackers, can monitor respiratory rate, oxygen saturation, heart rate, and physical activity levels.
- Data Tracking: Continuous data tracking allows for early detection of changes in respiratory status, facilitating prompt intervention and preventing exacerbations.

Patient Engagement

- Motivation: Wearable devices can motivate patients to adhere to treatment plans and engage in healthy behaviors by providing real-time feedback and progress tracking.

- Customization: Personalized alerts and reminders can be set to prompt medication adherence, exercise, and other self-management activities.

Mobile Health Applications

Symptom Tracking

- Apps: Mobile health applications designed for respiratory conditions allow patients to log symptoms, track medication usage, and monitor peak flow readings.
- Insights: These apps provide valuable insights into disease patterns and triggers, helping patients and healthcare providers tailor management plans.

Education and Support

- Resources: Mobile apps offer educational resources, including articles, videos, and interactive tools, to help patients better understand their condition and treatment options.
- Community: Many apps include community features, allowing patients to connect with others who have similar conditions, share experiences, and receive support.

Advanced Diagnostics

Artificial Intelligence (AI) and Machine Learning

- Early Detection: AI algorithms can analyze large datasets from electronic health records, imaging studies, and wearable devices to identify early signs of bronchitis and predict exacerbations.
- Personalized Medicine: Machine learning models can help tailor treatment plans based on individual patient data, improving outcomes and reducing adverse effects.

Improved Imaging Techniques

- High-Resolution Imaging: Advances in imaging technology, such as high-resolution computed tomography (HRCT) and functional magnetic resonance imaging (fMRI), provide detailed views of the airways and lung tissue, aiding in accurate diagnosis and monitoring.
- AI Integration: AI-enhanced imaging tools can assist radiologists in identifying subtle changes in lung structure and function, improving diagnostic accuracy and treatment planning.

Digital Therapeutics

Interactive Programs

- Behavioral Interventions: Digital therapeutics involve interactive programs that deliver evidence-based behavioral interventions to help patients manage bronchitis symptoms and improve health outcomes.
- Gamification: Gamified elements, such as rewards and challenges, can increase patient engagement and adherence to therapeutic programs.

Medication Management

- Adherence Tools: Digital platforms can provide medication reminders, track adherence, and offer educational content about prescribed treatments, ensuring patients follow their treatment plans accurately.
- Integration: Integration with electronic health records allows for seamless communication between patients and healthcare providers, enabling better management of medications and treatment adjustments.

Research and Development

Clinical Trials

- Virtual Trials: The use of technology in conducting virtual clinical trials allows for broader participation and more efficient data collection, accelerating the development of new treatments for bronchitis.
- Real-World Data: Wearable devices and mobile health apps provide real-world data that can enhance clinical research and improve understanding of disease progression and treatment effectiveness.

Technology is revolutionizing the management of bronchitis, offering new tools and methods to enhance diagnosis, treatment, and patient engagement. Healthcare providers must embrace these technological advancements to provide the best possible care for their patients. By integrating telemedicine, wearable devices, mobile health applications, advanced diagnostics, digital therapeutics, and ongoing research, the medical community can significantly improve outcomes for patients with bronchitis, ensuring they receive comprehensive, personalized, and efficient care.

DISCUSSION QUESTIONS

- . How has telemedicine changed the landscape of bronchitis care, and what are its benefits and limitations?
- Discuss the potential impact of wearable devices on the management of bronchitis, particularly in terms of patient monitoring and engagement

CONCLUSION

Bronchitis is a common respiratory condition that requires a comprehensive and multidisciplinary approach to management. This eBook has provided an extensive overview of bronchitis, tailored specifically for healthcare providers, including respiratory therapists, doctors, and nurses. By understanding the various aspects of bronchitis, from its clinical and physiological signs to diagnostic imaging, treatment options, and patient education, healthcare providers can enhance their ability to diagnose, treat, and manage this condition effectively. to advance our understanding and management of bronchitis. Emerging therapies, new diagnostic tools, and the potential of precision medicine hold promise for improving patient outcomes.

Healthcare providers must stay informed about these developments to offer cutting-edge care and educate patients about new treatment options. By integrating these advancements and focusing on prevention, Effective bronchitis management requires a holistic approach that combines medical knowledge, patient education, and the integration of new technologies. By fostering collaboration among healthcare providers and leveraging the latest advancements, we can improve the lives of patients with bronchitis. This eBook serves as a comprehensive guide to equip healthcare providers with the tools and knowledge necessary to deliver high-quality, patient-centered care. Together, we can make significant strides in the fight against bronchitis and ensure better health outcomes for all patients.

<u>REFERENCES</u>

- Barnes, P. J., & Drazen, J. M. (2002). *"Pathophysiology of Asthma." The New England Journal of Medicine.*
- Bousquet, J., Khaltaev, N., & Cruz, A. A. (2007). *"Global Surveillance, Prevention, and Control of Chronic Respiratory Diseases: A Comprehensive Approach." World Health Organization.*
- Busse, W. W., & Lemanske, R. F. (2001). *"Asthma." The New England Journal of Medicine.*
- Crofton, J., & Douglas, A. (2000). *"Respiratory Diseases." Blackwell Science.*
- Gibson, P. G., & Simpson, J. L. (2009). *"The Overlap Syndrome of Asthma and COPD: What Are Its Features and How Important is it?" Thorax.*
- Global Initiative for Chronic Obstructive Lung Disease (GOLD). (2020). *"Global Strategy for the Diagnosis, Management, and Prevention of COPD."*
- Hamid, Q., & Tulic, M. K. (2009). "Immunopathogenesis of Asthma.*" Annual Review of Physiology.*
- Hurst, J. R., & Wedzicha, J. A. (2004). *"Chronic Obstructive Pulmonary Disease: Management of Acute Exacerbations." Thorax.*
- Jeffery, P. K. (2004). *"Remodeling and Inflammation of Bronchi in Asthma and Chronic Obstructive Pulmonary Disease." Proceedings of the American Thoracic Society.*
- Koul, P. A. (2007). *"Chronic Obstructive Pulmonary Disease: Indian Guidelines and the Road Ahead." Lung India.*
- Mannino, D. M., & Buist, A. S. (2007). *"Global Burden of COPD: Risk Factors, Prevalence, and Future Trends." The Lancet.*

www.ingramcontent.com/pod-product-compliance
Lightning Source LLC
Chambersburg PA
CBHW072126150726
47999CB00005B/2144